Revolution and Romanticism, 1789-1834
*A series of facsimile reprints chosen and introduced by*
**Jonathan Wordsworth**
*University Lecturer in Romantic Studies at Oxford*

Hazlitt
**My first acquaintance with poets** 1823

William Hazlitt

# My first
# acquaintance
# with poets

1823

Woodstock Books
*Oxford and New York*
1993

This edition first published 1993 by
**Woodstock Books**
Spelsbury House, Spelsbury, Oxford OX7 3JR
and
Woodstock Books
387 Park Avenue South
New York, NY 10016-8810

ISBN 1 85477 129 9

**British Library Cataloguing in Publication Data**
A catalogue record for this book is
available from the British Library

**Library of Congress Cataloging-in-Publication Data**
Hazlitt, William, 1778-1830.
My first acquaintance with poets/William Hazlitt.
    p. cm. — (Revolution and romanticism, 1789-1834)
Originally published: The liberal. vol. 2. 1823.
ISBN 1-85477-129-9: $35.00
I. Hazlitt, William, 1778-1830—Friends and associates.
2. Wordsworth, William, 1770-1850—Friends and associates.
3. Coleridge, Samuel Taylor, 1772-1834—Friends and
associates. 4. Authors, English— 19th century—Biography. 5.
Poets, English— 19th century—Biography. I. Title. II. Series.
PR4773.A435    1993
821'.709—dc20                                                    93-17428
[B]                                                                    CIP

Printed and bound in Great Britain by
Smith Settle
Otley, West Yorkshire LS21 3JP

# Introduction

Perhaps *My first acquaintance with poets*, published in the *Liberal* in April 1823 and never 'collected' by Hazlitt himself, is really the best of all his essays. It is a big claim. No other English writer — not Addison, nor Johnson, nor Lamb, nor Pater — has produced so many that are masterpieces. *My first acquaintance* treats a subject of compelling interest, and treats it with more than customary brilliance. Recollections of Coleridge and Wordsworth such as are nowhere else to be found mingle with personal insights, personal asides, that enrich the texture of the prose, and our knowledge of three great writers.

Hazlitt the romantic nineteen-year-old who met Coleridge at Wem in January 1798 (and was then, four months later, introduced by him to Wordsworth and his sister at Nether Stowey) is envied, and affectionately mocked, by the sadder, wiser, older, self of 1823:

During those months the chill breath of winter gave me a welcoming; the vernal air was balm and inspiration to me. The golden sun-sets, the silver star of evening, lighted me on my way to new hopes and prospects. I was to visit *Coleridge in the spring*. (pp.35-6)

*My first acquaintance* is pervaded by this tender irony. Hazlitt permits himself in this essay something close to nostalgia: 'I had a sound in my ears, it was the voice of Fancy: I had a light before me, it was the face of Poetry. The one still lingers there, the other has not quitted my side' (p.35).

Audible at times, though, beneath these assertions of harmony is the voice of disappointment, offering a sort of bitter undersong. 'I observed', writes Hazlitt of Coleridge the walking companion,

that he continually crossed me on the way by shifting from one side of the footpath to the other. This struck me as an odd movement; but I did not at that time connect it with any instability of purpose or involuntary change of principle, as I have done since. (p.32)

The discourse upon noses contains another such undersinging, or undermining. Wordsworth has 'an intense high narrow forehead, a Roman nose, cheeks furrowed by strong purpose and feeling'. He has let no one down, and you can see it in his face. Not so Coleridge: 'His forehead was broad and high, light as if built of ivory, with large projecting eyebrows, and his eyes rolling beneath them like a sea with darkened lustre'.

So far so good: Coleridge may be a touch Satanic, his eyes reminiscent of the darkening Lucifer, but the portrait is strong and flattering. Hazlitt's painterly gaze moves on down Coleridge's face: 'His mouth was gross, voluptuous, open, eloquent [Hardly generous, though the last word strives to make amends!], his chin good humoured and round [Kindly meant, perhaps?], but his nose, the rudder of the face, the index of the will, was small, feeble, nothing – like what he has done' (p.27). No rudder, no will, no achievement. As in his review of the *Christabel* volume (1816), and his brilliant later essay in *Spirit of the age* (1825), Hazlitt refuses to perceive the grandeur of what has been achieved, because his former self had expected so much more. Partly it was Coleridge's own fault, for the making and breaking of promises. But Hazlitt, one feels, when faced with quality so astonishing, should have known better than to ask for quantity as well. The poet of the *Ancient mariner, Kubla Khan* and *Christabel* might have been forgiven a weak nose. If, that is, fallen idols could ever be forgiven.

'As we passed along', Hazlitt writes, 'between Wem and Shrewsbury ... a sound was in my ears as of a Siren's song' (pp.23-4). Hoping to become minister of the Unitarian congregation, Coleridge had preached that morning at Shrewsbury, 'like an eagle dallying with the wind' (p.25). Hazlitt had walked ten winter miles to hear him: 'I was stunned, startled with it', he recalled, 'as from deep sleep ... the light of his genius shone into my soul, like the sun's rays glittering in the puddles of the road' (p.24). Hazlitt's style has all its usual genius, but this time there is a personal quality that belongs to the sad and special year in which he is writing:

My soul has indeed remained in its original bondage, dark, obscure, with longings infinite and unsatisfied; my heart, shut up in the prison house of this rude clay, has never found, nor will it ever find, a heart to speak to; but that my understanding also did not remain dumb and brutish, or at length found a language to express itself, I owe to Coleridge. (p.24)

In early May 1823 — less than a month after *My first acquaintance with poets* – appeared Hazlitt's execrated 'Book of Love'. Sarah Walker, landlady's daughter, and not above sitting on a lodger's knee and kissing him, had been for Hazlitt the new Pygmalion, an ideal created from his yearnings for 'a heart to speak to':

To be with her is to be at peace. I have no other wish or desire. The air about her is serene, blissful; and he who breathes it is like one of the Gods! So that I can but have her with me always, I care for nothing more. I never could tire of her sweetness; I feel that I could grow to her, body and soul. My heart, my heart is hers.
(*Liber amoris*, 66)

Looking back to January 1798, Hazlitt records the appearance on the scene of the man who was his first idol, as well as the first poet of his acquaintance. His feelings veer between gratefulness and disappointment. Like Sarah, Coleridge had been partly Hazlitt's own creation, and was certain to let him down. Yet just as he had received from Sarah the chance – even perhaps the ability – to love, so he ascribes to Coleridge's inspiration the precious gift of language. There is a marvellous appropriateness in his having seen Coleridge first in the pulpit. Even the text he had chosen was guaranteed to impress:

When I got there, the organ was playing the 100th psalm, and, when it was done, Mr Coleridge rose and gave out his text, 'And he went up into the mountain to pray, HIMSELF, ALONE.' As he gave out this text, his voice 'rose like a steam of rich distilled perfumes', and when he came to the two last words, which he pronounced loud, deep, and distinct, it seemed to me, who was then young, as if the sounds had echoed from the bottom of the human heart, and as if that prayer might have floated in solemn silence through the universe. (p.25)

Arriving at Nether Stowey, Hazlitt is taken by Coleridge to Alfoxden and the new world of *Lyrical ballads*. Dorothy gets them a meal ('a frugal repast'), and he is permitted to browse among manuscripts, now lost, of all Wordsworth's major ballads, together with the *Ancient mariner*, and presumably *Christabel* Part I. Seated with Coleridge 'on the trunk of an old ash-tree that stretched along the ground', he makes the acquaintance of his second poet through a reading of 'the ballad of *Betty Foy*'. That he should have retitled the *Idiot boy* in his mind, putting emphasis on Betty Foy rather than Johnny, is perhaps significant. Wordsworth's tender comedy he takes for granted. It is in the *Thorn, Mad mother* and *Forsaken indian woman* that he feels the 'deeper power and pathos' which prompted him to greet a new movement in English poetry. 'The sense', he writes memorably,

of a new style and a new spirit in poetry came over me. It had to me something of the effect that arises from the turning up of the fresh soil, or of the first welcome breath of Spring, 'While yet the trembling year is unconfirmed'. (p.39)

Wordsworth's arrival in the flesh, 'gaunt and Don Quixote-like' and 'dressed (according to the *costume* of that unconstrained period) in a brown fustian jacket and striped pantaloons', has been a joy to biographers, as have his 'northern *burr,* like the crust on wine' and the 'havoc' he makes 'of the half of a Cheshire cheese'. Though his poetry is from the first more important to Hazlitt than Coleridge's, Wordsworth's role is less significant. We see him in *My first acquaintance* more externally, more anecdotally. There is the nice touch as he looks out of 'the low, latticed window' and remarks on the sunset, and Hazlitt (the twenty-year-old) thinks within himself, 'With what eyes these poets see nature' (p.40). And there is the open-air reading of *Peter Bell*, 'very different from that of some later critics' (p.41). But apart from his disparagement of the *Castle spectre* – 'it fitted the taste of the audience like a glove' (p.40) – there are none of the telling observations and turns of phrase that Hazlitt has stored up from Coleridge: Mackintosh, as 'the ready warehouseman of letters' (p.30), or Pope and his fellow couplet-writers, whose 'ears ... might be charged with having short memories, that could not retain the harmony of whole passages' (p.44).

Sidelights on Wordsworth come either courtesy of Coleridge, or through comparisons that Hazlitt sets up between his two poet acquaintances. Oddest is surely Coleridge's much quoted remark about 'clinging to the palpable'.

He lamented that Wordsworth was not prone enough to belief in the traditional superstitions of the place, and that there was a something corporeal, a *matter-of-factness*, a clinging to the palpable, or often to the petty, in his poetry, in consequence. His genius was not a spirit that descended to him through the air; it sprung out of the ground like a flower, or unfolded itself from a green spray, on which the goldfinch sang. (p.39).

What did Coleridge really say? Given the beautiful second sentence, how critical did he intend to be? Why should matter-of-factness be blamed on failure to believe in local superstitions? Had not Wordsworth in the previous weeks based three major ballads (*Goody Blake and Harry Gill*, the *Thorn* and *Peter Bell*) precisely on the workings of superstitious minds? Compelling as it is, the story has an air of being slightly garbled.

Not so Hazlitt's brilliant recollections of the two poets' modes of reading and composition. First the sharper touch that tickles them both:

There is a *chaunt* in the recitation both of Coleridge and Wordsworth, which acts as a spell upon the hearer, and disarms the judgment. Perhaps they have deceived themselves by making habitual use of this ambiguous accompaniment.

Then the distinctions that we wish to have made:

Coleridge's manner is more full, animated, and varied; Wordsworth's more equable, sustained, and internal. The one might be termed more *dramatic*, the other more *lyrical*.

Finally, the bonne-bouche, as Hazlitt moves into the half symbolic mode of story-telling that he specially enjoys:

Coleridge has told me that he himself liked to compose in walking over uneven ground, or breaking through the straggling branches of a copsewood; where Wordsworth always wrote (if he could) walking up and down a strait gravel walk, or in some spot where the continuity of his verse met with no collateral interruption. (p.41)

In an essay that is pleasure from start to finish, no two readers will recall the same delights. Wordsworth's pantaloons (what colour, one wonders, were the stripes?) gain a place in literary history that no one could have predicted. There may just be a place too for John Chester, bow-legged, with 'a drag in his walk like a drover', who 'kept on a sort of trot by the side of Coleridge, like a running footman by a state coach, that he might not lose a syllable or sound, that fell from (his) lips' (p.42). The thought of Coleridge crossing from side to side in the young Hazlitt's path has an imaginative rightness: it is how we wish to be. Less certain to be noticed is the moment of decision. Hearing in Shropshire of the Wedgwoods' offer of an annuity that would free him from the need to take a job, Coleridge has suddenly to choose between his two callings – preacher or poet? Can he turn down the prospect of becoming a Unitarian minister when he has won such golden opinions from the congregation at Shrewsbury? Hazlitt, who can still recall the disappointment involved for his youthful self, records in level tones: 'Coleridge seemed to make up his mind to close with [the Wedgwoods'] proposal in the act of tying on one of his shoes' (p.31).

J.W.

# THE

# LIBERAL.

## VERSE AND PROSE FROM THE

## SOUTH.

———————

### VOLUME THE SECOND.

———————

LONDON, 1823:

PRINTED FOR JOHN HUNT,

22, OLD BOND STREET.

LONDON:

PRINTED BY C. H. REYNELL, BROAD STREET, GOLDEN SQUARE.

# CONTENTS.

# MY FIRST ACQUAINTANCE WITH POETS.

My father was a Dissenting Minister at W——m in Shrop-shire; and in the year 1798 (the figures that compose that date are to me like the " dreaded name of Demogorgon") Mr. Coleridge came to Shrewsbury, to succeed Mr. Rowe in the spiritual charge of a Unitarian Congregation there.   He did not come till late on the Saturday afternoon before he was to preach;   and Mr. Rowe, who himself went down to the coach in a state of anxiety and expectation, to look for the arrival of his successor, could find no one at all answering the description  but a round-faced man in a short black coat (like a shooting-jacket) which hardly seemed to have been made for him, but who seemed to be talking at a great rate to his fellow-passengers.   Mr. Rowe had scarce returned to give an account of his disappointment, when the round-faced man in black entered, and dissipated all doubts on the subject, by beginning to talk.   He did not cease while he staid;   nor has he since, that I know of.   He held the good town of Shrews-bury in delightful suspense for three weeks that he remained there, " fluttering the *proud Salopians* like an eagle in a dove-cote;" and the Welch mountains that skirt the horizon with their tempestuous confusion, agree to have heard no such mystic sounds since the days of

> " High-born Hoel's harp or soft Llewellyn's lay !"

As we passed along between W——m and Shrewsbury, and I eyed their blue tops seen through the wintry branches, or the red rustling leaves of the sturdy oak-trees by the road-side, a sound was in my ears as of a Siren's song; I was stunned, startled with it, as from deep sleep; but I had no notion then that I should ever be able to express my admiration to others in motley imagery or quaint allusion, till the light of his genius shone into my soul, like the sun's rays glittering in the puddles of the road. I was at that time dumb, inarticulate, helpless, like a worm by the way-side, crushed, bleeding, lifeless; but now, bursting from the deadly bands that "bound them,

> "With Styx nine times round them,"

my ideas float on winged words, and as they expand their plumes, catch the golden light of other years. My soul has indeed remained in its original bondage, dark, obscure, with longings infinite and unsatisfied; my heart, shut up in the prison-house of this rude clay, has never found, nor will it ever find, a heart to speak to; but that my understanding also did not remain dumb and brutish, or at length found a language to express itself, I owe to Coleridge. But this is not to my purpose.

My father lived ten miles from Shrewsbury, and was in the habit of exchanging visits with Mr Rowe, and with Mr. Jenkins of Whitchurch (nine miles farther on) according to the custom of Dissenting Ministers in each other's neighbourhood. A line of communication is thus established, by which the flame of civil and religious liberty is kept alive, and nourishes its smouldering fire unquenchable, like the fires in the Agamemnon of Æschylus, placed at different stations, that waited for ten long years to announce with their blazing pyramids the destruction of Troy. Coleridge had agreed to come over to see my father, according to the courtesy of the country, as Mr. Rowe's probable successor; but in the mean time I had gone to hear him preach the Sunday after his arrival. A poet and a philosopher getting up into a Unitarian pulpit to preach the Gospel, was a romance in these degenerate days, a sort of revival of the primitive spirit of Christianity, which was not to be resisted.

It was in January, 1798, that I rose one morning before day-light, to walk ten miles in the mud, and went to hear this celebrated person preach. Never, the longest day I have to live, shall I have such another walk as this cold, raw, comfortless one, in the winter of the year 1798.— *Il y a des impressions que ni le tems ni les circonstances peuvent effacer. Dussé-je vivre des siècles entiers, le doux tems de ma jeunesse ne peut renaitre pour moi, ni s'effacer jamais dans ma mémoire.* When I got there, the organ was playing the 100th psalm, and, when it was done, Mr. Coleridge rose and gave out his text, " And he went up into the mountain to pray, HIMSELF, ALONE." As he gave out this text, his voice " rose like a steam of rich distilled perfumes," and when he came to the two last words, which he pronounced loud, deep, and distinct, it seemed to me, who was then young, as if the sounds had echoed from the bottom of the human heart, and as if that prayer might have floated in solemn silence through the universe. The idea of St. John came into mind, " of one crying in the wilderness, who had his loins girt about, and whose food was locusts and wild honey." The preacher then launched into his subject, like an eagle dallying with the wind. The sermon was upon peace and war; upon church and state—not their alliance, but their separation—on the spirit of the world and the spirit of Christianity, not as the same, but as opposed to one another. He talked of those who had " inscribed the cross of Christ on banners dripping with human gore." He made a poetical and pastoral excursion,—and to shew the fatal effects of war, drew a striking contrast between the simple shepherd boy, driving his team afield, or sitting under the hawthorn, piping to his flock, "as though he should never be old," and the same poor country-lad, crimped, kidnapped, brought into town, made drunk at an alehouse, turned into a wretched drummer-boy, with his hair sticking on end with powder and pomatum, a long cue at his back, and tricked out in the loathsome finery of the profession of blood.

> "Such were the notes our once-lov'd poet sung."

And for myself, I could not have been more delighted if I had heard the music of the spheres. Poetry and Philosophy had met together, Truth and Genius had embraced, under the eye and with the sanction of Religion. This was even beyond my hopes   I returned home well satisfied. The sun that was still labouring pale and wan through the sky, obscured by thick mists, seemed an emblem of the *good cause;* and the cold dank drops of dew that hung half melted on the beard of the thistle, had something genial and refreshing in them; for there was a spirit of hope and youth in all nature, that turned every thing into good. The face of nature had not then the brand of Jus Divinum on it:

> "Like to that sanguine flower inscrib'd with woe."

On the Tuesday following, the half-inspired speaker came. I was called down into the room where he was, and went half-hoping, half-afraid. He received me very graciously, and I listened for a long time without uttering a word. I did not suffer in his opinion by my silence. "For those two hours," he afterwards was pleased to say, "he was conversing with W. H.'s forehead!" His appearance was different from what I had anticipated from seeing him before. At a

distance, and in the dim light of the chapel, there was to me
a strange wildness in his aspect, a dusky obscurity, and I
thought him pitted with the small-pox. His complexion
was at that time clear, and even bright—

> " As are the children of yon azure sheen."

His forehead was broad and high, light as if built of ivory,
with large projecting eyebrows, and his eyes rolling beneath
them like a sea with darkened lustre. " A certain tender
bloom his face o'erspread," a purple tinge as we see it in
the pale thoughtful complexions of the Spanish portrait-
painters, Murillo and Velasquez. His mouth was gross, voluptuous, open, eloquent; his chin good-humoured and
round; but his nose, the rudder of the face, the index of the
will, was small, feeble, nothing—like what he has done. It
might seem that the genius of his face as from a height
surveyed and projected him (with sufficient capacity and
huge aspiration) into the world unknown of thought and
imagination, with nothing to support or guide his veering
purpose, as if Columbus had launched his adventurous
course for the New World in a scallop, without oars or com-
pass. So at least I comment on it after the event. Coleridge in his person was rather above the common size, in-
clining to the corpulent, or like Lord Hamlet, " somewhat
fat and pursy." His hair (now, alas! grey) was then black
and glossy as the raven's, and fell in smooth masses over his
forehead. This long pendulous hair is peculiar to enthu-
siasts, to those whose minds tend heavenward; and is tra-
ditionally inseparable (though of a different colour) from
the pictures of Christ. It ought to belong, as a character,
to all who preach *Christ crucified*, and Coleridge was at that
time one of those!

It was curious to observe the contrast between him and

my father, who was a veteran in the cause, and then declin-
ing into the vale of years.   He had been a poor Irish lad,
carefully brought up by his parents, and sent to the University of Glasgow (where he studied under Adam Smith) to
prepare him for his future destination.   It was his mother's
proudest wish to see her son a Dissenting Minister.   So if
we look back to past generations (as far as eye can reach)
we see the same hopes, fears, wishes, followed by the same
disappointments, throbbing in the human heart; and so we
may see them (if we look forward) rising up for ever, and
disappearing, like vapourish bubbles, in the human breast!
After being tossed about from congregation to congregation
in the heats of the Unitarian controversy, and squabbles
about the American war, he had been relegated to an obscure village, where he was to spend the last thirty years of
his life, far from the only converse that he loved, the talk
about disputed texts of Scripture and the cause of civil and
religious liberty.   Here he passed his days, repining but re-,
signed, in the study of the Bible, and the perusal of the Com-
mentators,—huge folios, not easily got through, one of which
would outlast a winter!   Why did he pore on these from
morn to night (with the exception of a walk in the fields or
a turn in the garden to gather brocoli-plants or kidney-
beans of his own rearing, with no small degree of pride and
pleasure)?—Here were " no figures nor no fantasies,"—neither poetry nor philosophy—nothing to dazzle, nothing to
excite modern curiosity;  but to his lack-lustre eyes there
appeared, within the pages of the ponderous, unwieldy, ne-
glected tomes, the sacred name of JEHOVAH in Hebrew
capitals: pressed down by the weight of the style, worn to the
last fading thinness of the understanding, there were glimpses,
glimmering notions of the patriarchal wanderings, with palm-
trees hovering in the horizon, and processions of camels at

the distance of three thousand years; there was Moses with the Burning Bush, the number of the Twelve Tribes, types, shadows, glosses on the law and the prophets; there were discussions (dull enough) on the age of Methuselah, a mighty speculation! there were outlines, rude guesses at the shape of Noah's Ark and of the riches of Solomon's Temple; questions as to the date of the creation, predictions of the end of all things; the great lapses of time, the strange mutations of the globe were unfolded with the voluminous leaf, as it turned over; and though the soul might slumber with an hieroglyphic veil of inscrutable mysteries drawn over it, yet it was in a slumber ill-exchanged for all the sharpened realities of sense, wit, fancy, or reason.   My father's life was comparatively a dream; but it was a dream of infinity and eternity, of death, the resurrection, and a judgment to come !

No two individuals were ever more unlike than were the host and his guest.   A poet was to my father a sort of non-descript: yet whatever added grace to the Unitarian cause was to him welcome.   He could hardly have been more surprised or pleased, if our visitor had worn wings.   Indeed, his thoughts had wings; and as the silken sounds rustled round our little wainscoted parlour, my father threw back his spectacles over his forehead, his white hairs mixing with its sanguine hue; and a smile of delight beamed across his rugged cordial face, to think that Truth had found a new ally in Fancy ! *   Besides, Coleridge seemed to take considerable notice of me, and that of itself was enough.   He talked very

---

* My father was one of those who mistook his talent after all.   He used to be very much dissatisfied that I preferred his Letters to his Sermons.   The last were forced and dry; the first came naturally from him.   For ease, half-plays on words, and a supine, monkish, indolent pleasantry, I have never seen them equalled.

familiarly, but agreeably, and glanced over a variety of sub-
jects.   At dinner-time he grew more animated, and dilated
in a very edifying manner on Mary Wolstonecraft and Mackintosh.   The last, he said, he considered (on my father's
speaking of his *Vindiciæ Gallicæ* as a capital performance)
as a clever scholastic man—a master of the topics,—or as
the ready warehouseman of letters, who knew exactly where
to lay his hand on what he wanted, though the goods were
not his own.   He thought him no match for Burke, either
in style or matter.   Burke was a metaphysician, Mackintosh
a mere logician.   Burke was an orator (almost a poet) who
reasoned in figures, because he had an eye for nature :  Mackintosh, on the other hand, was a rhetorician, who had only
an eye to common-places.   On this I ventured to say that
I had always entertained a great opinion of Burke, and that
(as far as I could find) the speaking of him with contempt
might be made the test of a vulgar democratical mind.   This
was the first observation I ever made to Coleridge, and he
said it was a very just and striking one.   I remember the leg
of Welsh mutton and the turnips on the table that day had
the finest flavour imaginable.   Coleridge added that Mackintosh and Tom. Wedgwood (of whom, however, he spoke
highly) had expressed a very indifferent opinion of his friend
Mr. Wordsworth, on which he remarked to them—" He
strides on so far before you, that he dwindles in the distance!"
Godwin had once boasted to him of having carried on an
argument with Mackintosh for three hours with dubious suc-
cess ; Coleridge told him—" If there had been a man of
genius in the room, he would have settled the question in
five minutes."   He asked me if I had ever seen Mary Wolstonecraft, and I said, I had once for a few moments, and
that she seemed to me to turn off Godwin's objections to
something she advanced with quite a playful, easy air.   He

replied, that " this was only one instance of the ascendancy which people of imagination exercised over those of mere intellect." He did not rate Godwin very high * (this was caprice or prejudice, real or affected) but he had a great idea of Mrs. Wolstonecraft's powers of conversation, none at all of her talent for book-making. We talked a little about Holcroft. He had been asked if he was not much struck *with* him, and he said, he thought himself in more danger of being struck *by* him. I complained that he would not let me get on at all, for he required a definition of every the commonest word, exclaiming, " What do you mean by a *sensation*, Sir? What do you mean by an *idea?*" This, Coleridge said, was barricadoing the road to truth :—it was setting up a turnpike-gate at every step we took. I forget a great number of things, many more than I remember; but the day passed off pleasantly, and the next morning Mr. Coleridge was to return to Shrewsbury. When I came down to breakfast, I found that he had just received a letter from his friend, T. Wedgwood, making him an offer of £150. a-year if he chose to wave his present pursuit, and devote himself entirely to the study of poetry and philosophy. Coleridge seemed to make up his mind to close with this proposal in the act of tying on one of his shoes. It threw an additional damp on his departure. It took the wayward enthusiast quite from us to cast him into Deva's winding vales, or by the shores of old romance. Instead of living at ten miles distance, of being the pastor of a Dissenting congregation at Shrewsbury, he was henceforth to inhabit the

---

* He complained in particular of the presumption of his attempting to establish the future immortality of man, " without" (as he said) " knowing what Death was or what Life was"—and the tone in which he pronounced these two words seemed to convey a complete image of both.

Hill of Parnassus, to be a Shepherd on the Delectable Mountains. Alas! I knew not the way thither, and felt very little gratitude for Mr. Wedgwood's bounty. I was presently relieved from this dilemma; for Mr. Coleridge, asking for a pen and ink, and going to a table to write something on a bit of card, advanced towards me with undulating step, and giving me the precious document, said that that was his address, *Mr. Coleridge, Nether-Stowey, Somersetshire;* and that he should be glad to see me there in a few weeks' time, and, if I chose, would come half-way to meet me. I was not less surprised than the shepherd-boy (this simile is to be found in Cassandra) when he sees a thunder-bolt fall close at his feet. I stammered out my acknowledgments and acceptance of this offer (I thought Mr. Wedgwood's annuity a trifle to it) as well as I could; and this mighty business being settled, the poet-preacher took leave, and I accompanied him six miles on the road. It was a fine morning in the middle of winter, and he talked the whole way. The scholar in Chaucer is described as going

—— " Sounding on his way."

So Coleridge went on his. In digressing, in dilating, in passing from subject to subject, he appeared to me to float in air, to slide on ice. He told me in confidence (going along) that he should have preached two sermons before he accepted the situation at Shrewsbury, one on Infant Baptism, the other on the Lord's Supper, shewing that he could not administer either, which would have effectually disqualified him for the object in view. I observed that he continually crossed me on the way by shifting from one side of the foot-path to the other. This struck me as an odd movement; but I did not at that time connect it with any instability of purpose or involuntary change of principle, as I have done since. He

seemed unable to keep on in a strait line.   He spoke slight-
ingly of Hume (whose Essay on Miracles he said was stolen
from an objection started in one of South's Sermons—*Credat
Judæus Apella!*).   I was not very much pleased at this account of Hume, for I had just been reading, with infinite
relish, that completest of all metaphysical *choke-pears,* his
*Treatise on Human Nature,* to which the *Essays,* in point
of scholastic subtlety and close reasoning, are mere elegant
trifling, light summer-reading.   Coleridge even denied the
excellence of Hume's general style, which I think betrayed
a want of taste or candour.   He however made me amends
by the manner in which he spoke of Berkeley.   He dwelt
particularly on his *Essay on Vision* as a masterpiece of ana-
lytical reasoning.   So it undoubtedly is.   He was exceed-
ingly angry with Dr. Johnson for striking the stone with his
foot, in allusion to this author's Theory of Matter and Spirit,
and saying, " Thus I confute him, Sir."   Coleridge drew a
parallel (I don't know how he brought about the connection)
between Bishop Berkeley and Tom Paine.   He said the one
was an instance of a subtle, the other of an acute mind, than
which no two things could be more distinct.   The one was a
shop-boy's quality, the other the characteristic of a philosopher.   He considered Bishop Butler as a true philosopher, a
profound and conscientious thinker, a genuine reader of nature
and of his own mind.   He did not speak of his *Analogy,* but of
his *Sermons at the Rolls' Chapel,* of which I had never heard.
Coleridge somehow always contrived to prefer the *unknown* to
the *known.*   In this instance he was right.   The *Analogy* is a
tissue of sophistry, of wire-drawn, theological special-plead-
ing; the *Sermons* (with the Preface to them) are in a fine
vein of deep, matured reflection, a candid appeal to our observation of human nature, without pedantry and without
bias. I told Coleridge I had written a few remarks, and was

sometimes foolish enough to believe that I had made a discovery on the same subject (the *Natural Disinterestedness
of the Human Mind)*—and I tried to explain my view of it to
Coleridge, who listened with great willingness, but I did not
succeed in making myself understood. I sat down to the
task shortly afterwards for the twentieth time, got new pens
and paper, determined to make clear work of it, wrote a few
meagre sentences in the skeleton-style of a mathematical
demonstration, stopped half-way down the second page; and,
after trying in vain to pump up any words, images, notions,
apprehensions, facts, or observations, from that gulph of
abstraction in which I had plunged myself for four or five
years preceding, gave up the attempt as labour in vain, and
shed tears of helpless despondency on the blank unfinished
paper. I can write fast enough now. Am I better than I was
then? Oh no! One truth discovered, one pang of regret
at not being able to express it, is better than all the fluency
and flippancy in the world. Would that I could go back to
what I then was! Why can we not revive past times as we
can revisit old places? If I had the quaint Muse of Sir Philip
Sidney to assist me, I would write a *Sonnet to the Road
between W—m and Shrewsbury,* and immortalise every step
of it by some fond enigmatical conceit. I would swear that
the very milestones had ears, and that Harmer-hill stooped
with all its pines, to listen to a poet, as he passed! I remember but one other topic of discourse in this walk. He men-
tioned Paley, praised the naturalness and clearness of his
style, but condemned his sentiments, thought him a mere
time-serving casuist, and said that " the fact of his work on
Moral and Political Philosophy being made a text-book in
our Universities was a disgrace to the national character."
We parted at the six-mile stone; and I returned homeward,
pensive but much pleased. I had met with unexpected

notice from a person, whom I believed to have been prejudiced against me.    " Kind and affable to me had been
his condescension, and should be honoured ever with suit-
able regard."    He was the first poet I had known, and
he certainly answered to that inspired name.    I had heard a
great deal of his powers of conversation, and was not disap-
pointed.    In fact, I never met with any thing at all like
them, either before or since.    I could easily credit the ac-
counts which were circulated of his holding forth to a large
party of ladies and gentlemen, an evening or two before, on
the Berkeleian Theory, when he made the whole material
universe look like a transparency of fine words ; and another
story (which I believe he has somewhere told himself) of
his being asked to a party at Birmingham, of his smoking
tobacco and going to sleep after dinner on a sofa, where
the company found him to their no small surprise, which
was increased to wonder when he started up of a sudden,
and rubbing his eyes, looked about him, and launched into a
three-hours' description of the third heaven, of which he had
had a dream, very different from Mr. Southey's Vision of
Judgment, and also from that other Vision of Judgment,
which Mr. Murray, the Secretary of the Bridge-street Junto,
has taken into his especial keeping !

On my way back, I had a sound in my ears, it was the
voice of Fancy : I had a light before me, it was the face of
Poetry.    The one still lingers there, the other has not quitted my side !    Coleridge in truth met me half-way on the
ground of philosophy, or I should not have been won over
to his imaginative creed.    I had an uneasy, pleasurable sensation all the time, till I was to visit him.    During those
months the chill breath of winter gave me a welcoming ; the
vernal air was balm and inspiration to me.    The golden
sun-sets, the silver star of evening, lighted me on my way to

new hopes and prospects. *I was to visit Coleridge in the Spring.* This circumstance was never absent from my thoughts, and mingled with all my feelings. I wrote to him at the time proposed, and received an answer postponing my intended visit for a week or two, but very cordially urging me to complete my promise then. This delay did not damp, but rather increase my ardour. In the mean time, I went to Llangollen Vale, by way of initiating myself in the mysteries of natural scenery; and I must say I was enchanted with it. I had been reading Coleridge's description of England, in his fine *Ode on the Departing Year,* and I applied it, *con amore,* to the objects before me. That valley was to me (in a manner) the cradle of a new existence : in the river that winds through it, my spirit was baptised in the waters of Helicon!

I returned home, and soon after set out on my journey with unworn heart and untried feet. My way lay through Worcester and Gloucester, and by Upton, where I thought of Tom Jones and the adventure of the muff. I remember getting completely wet through one day, and stopping at an inn (I think it was at Tewkesbury) where I sat up all night to read Paul and Virginia. Sweet were the showers in early youth that drenched my body, and sweet the drops of pity that fell upon the books I read! I recollect a remark of Coleridge's upon this very book, that nothing could shew the gross indelicacy of French manners and the entire corruption of their imagination more strongly than the behaviour of the heroine in the last fatal scene, who turns away from a person on board the sinking vessel, that offers to save her life, because he has thrown off his clothes to assist him in swimming. Was this a time to think of such a circumstance ? I once hinted to Wordsworth, as we were sailing in his boat on Grasmere lake, that I thought he had borrowed the idea of his *Poems on the Naming of Places* from the local inscriptions of the same kind in Paul and Virginia. He did not own the obligation, and stated some distinction without a difference, in defence of his claim to originality. Any the slightest variation would be sufficient for this purpose in his mind; for whatever *he* added or omitted would inevitably be worth all that any one else had done, and contain the marrow of the sentiment.—I was still two days before the time fixed for my arrival, for I had taken care to set out early enough. I stopped these two days at Bridgewater, and when I was tired of sauntering on the banks of its muddy river, returned to the inn, and read Camilla. So have I loitered my life away, reading books, looking at pictures, going to plays, hearing, thinking, writing on what pleased me best. I have wanted only one thing to make me happy; but wanting that, have wanted every thing!

I arrived, and was well received. The country about Nether Stowey is beautiful, green and hilly, and near the sea-shore. I saw it but the other day, after an interval of twenty years, from a hill near Taunton. How was the map of my life spread out before me, as the map of the country lay at my feet! In the afternoon, Coleridge took me over to All-Foxden, a romantic old family-mansion of the St. Aubins, where Wordsworth lived. It was then in the possession of a friend of the poet's, who gave him the free use of it. Somehow that period (the time just after the French Revolution) was not a time when *nothing was given for nothing*. The mind opened, and a softness might be perceived coming over the heart of individuals, beneath " the scales that fence " our self-interest. Wordsworth himself was from home, but his sister kept house, and set before us a frugal repast; and we had free access to her brother's poems, the

*Lyrical Ballads,* which were still in manuscript, or in the
form of *Sybilline Leaves.* I dipped into a few of these with
great satisfaction, and with the faith of a novice. I slept
that night in an old room with blue hangings, and co-
vered with the round-faced family-portraits of the age of
George I. and II. and from the wooded declivity of the ad-
joining park that overlooked my window, at the dawn of
day, could

——— " hear the loud stag speak."

In the outset of life (and particularly at this time I felt it
so) our imagination has a body to it. We are in a state between sleeping and waking, and have indistinct but glorious
glimpses of strange shapes, and there is always something
to come better than what we see. As in our dreams the ful-
ness of the blood gives warmth and reality to the coinage of
the brain, so in youth our ideas are clothed, and fed, and
pampered with our good spirits; we breathe thick with
thoughtless happiness, the weight of future years presses on
the strong pulses of the heart, and we repose with undis-
turbed faith in truth and good. As we advance, we exhaust
our fund of enjoyment and of hope. We are no longer
wrapped in *lamb's-wool,* lulled in Elysium. As we taste the
pleasures of life, their spirit evaporates, the sense palls; and
nothing is left but the phantoms, the lifeless shadows of what
*has been!*

That morning, as soon as breakfast was over, we strolled
out into the park, and seating ourselves on the trunk of an
old ash-tree that stretched along the ground, Coleridge read
aloud with a sonorous and musical voice, the ballad of *Betty
Foy.* I was not critically or sceptically inclined. I saw
touches of truth and nature, and took the rest for granted.

But in the *Thorn*, the *Mad Mother*, and the *Complaint of a Poor Indian Woman*, I felt that deeper power and pathos which have been since acknowledged,

> " In spite of pride, in erring reason's spite,"

as the characteristics of this author; and the sense of a new style and a new spirit in poetry came over me. It had to me something of the effect that arises from the turning up of the fresh soil, or of the first welcome breath of Spring,

> " While yet the trembling year is unconfirmed."

Coleridge and myself walked back to Stowey that evening, and his voice sounded high

> " Of Providence, foreknowledge, will, and fate,
> Fix'd fate, free-will, foreknowledge absolute,"

as we passed through echoing grove, by fairy stream or waterfall, gleaming in the summer moonlight! He lamented that Wordsworth was not prone enough to belief in the traditional superstitions of the place, and that there was a something corporeal, a *matter-of-fact-ness*, a clinging to the palpable, or often to the petty, in his poetry, in consequence. His genius was not a spirit that descended to him through the air; it sprung out of the ground like a flower, or unfolded itself from a green spray, on which the gold-finch sang. He said, however (if I remember right) that this objection must be confined to his descriptive pieces, that his philosophic poetry had a grand and comprehensive spirit in it, so that his soul seemed to inhabit the universe like a palace, and to discover truth by intuition, rather than by deduction. The next day Wordsworth arrived from Bristol at Coleridge's cottage. I think I see him now. He answered in some degree to his friend's description of him, but was more gaunt and Don Quixote-like. He was quaintly dressed (according to the *costume* of that unconstrained period) in a brown fustian jacket and striped pantaloons. There was something of a roll, a lounge in his gait, not unlike his own Peter Bell. There was a severe, worn pressure of thought about his temples, a fire in his eye (as if he saw something in objects more than the outward appearance) an intense high narrow forehead, a Roman nose, cheeks furrowed by strong purpose and feeling, and a convulsive inclination to laughter about the mouth, a good deal at variance with the solemn, stately expression of the rest of his face. Chantry's bust wants the marking traits; but he was teazed into making it regular and heavy: Haydon's head of him, introduced into the *Entrance of Christ into Jerusalem,* is the most like his drooping weight of thought and expression. He sat down and talked very naturally and freely, with a mixture of clear gushing accents in his voice, a deep guttural intonation, and a strong tincture of the northern *burr,* like the crust on wine. He instantly began to make havoc of the half of a Cheshire cheese on the table, and said triumphantly that " his marriage with experience had not been so unproductive as Mr. Southey's in teaching him a knowledge of the good things of this life." He had been to see the *Castle Spectre* by Monk Lewis, while at Bristol, and described it very well. He said " it fitted the taste of the audience like a glove." This *ad captandum* merit was however by no means a recommendation of it, according to the severe principles of the new school, which reject rather than court popular effect. Wordsworth, looking out of the low, latticed window, said, " How beautifully the sun sets on that yellow bank !" I thought within myself, " With what eyes these poets see nature !" and ever after, when I saw the sun-set stream upon the objects facing it, conceived I had made a

discovery, or thanked Mr. Wordsworth for having made one
for me! We went over to All-Foxden again the day following, and Wordsworth read us the story of Peter Bell in the
open air; and the comment made upon it by his face and voice
was very different from that of some later critics! Whatever
might be thought of the poem, "his face was as a book where
men might read strange matters," and he announced the fate
of his hero in prophetic tones.    There is a *chaunt* in the
recitation both of Coleridge and Wordsworth, which acts as
a spell upon the hearer, and disarms the judgment. Perhaps
they have deceived themselves by making habitual use of
this ambiguous accompaniment.    Coleridge's manner is
more full, animated, and varied; Wordsworth's more equable, sustained, and internal. The one might be termed more
*dramatic*, the other more *lyrical*.    Coleridge has told me
that he himself liked to compose in walking over uneven
ground, or breaking through the straggling branches of a
copsewood; whereas Wordsworth always wrote (if he could)
walking up and down a strait gravel-walk, or in some spot
where the continuity of his verse met with no collateral interruption.    Returning that same evening, I got into a
metaphysical argument with Wordsworth, while Coleridge
was explaining the different notes of the nightingale to his sister, in which we neither of us succeeded in making ourselves
perfectly clear and intelligible.    Thus I passed three weeks
at Nether Stowey and in the neighbourhood, generally de-
voting the afternoons to a delightful chat in an arbour made
of bark by the poet's friend Tom Poole, sitting under two
fine elm-trees, and listening to the bees humming round us,
while we quaffed our *flip*.    It was agreed, among other
things, that we should make a jaunt down the Bristol-Chan-
nel, as far as Linton. We set off together on foot, Coleridge, John Chester, and I. This Chester was a native of

Nether Stowey, one of those who were attracted to Coleridge's discourse as flies are to honey, or bees in swarming-time to the sound of a brass pan. He " followed in the chace, like a dog who hunts, not like one that made up the cry." He had on a brown cloth coat, boots, and corduroy breeches, was low in stature, bow-legged, had a drag in his walk like a drover, which he assisted by a hazel switch, and kept on a sort of trot by the side of Coleridge, like a running footman by a state coach, that he might not lose a syllable or sound, that fell from Coleridge's lips. He told me his private opinion, that Coleridge was a wonderful man. He scarcely opened his lips, much less offered an opinion the whole way: yet of the three, had I to chuse during that journey, I would be John Chester. He afterwards followed Coleridge into Germany, where the Kantean philosophers were puzzled how to bring him under any of their categories. When he sat down at table with his idol, John's felicity was complete; Sir Walter Scott's, or Mr. Blackwood's, when they sat down at the same table with the King, was not more so. We passed Dunster on our right, a small town between the brow of a hill and the sea. I remember eying it wistfully as it lay below us: contrasted with the woody scene around, it looked as clear, as pure, as *embrowned* and ideal as any landscape I have seen since, of Gaspar Poussin's or Domenichino's. We had a long day's march—(our feet kept time to the echoes of Coleridge's tongue)—through Minehead and by the Blue Anchor, and on to Linton, which we did not reach till near midnight, and where we had some difficulty in making a lodgment. We however knocked the people of the house up at last, and we were repaid for our apprehensions and fatigue by some excellent rashers of fried bacon and eggs. The view in coming along had been splendid. We walked for miles and miles on dark brown heaths overlooking the channel, with the Welsh hills beyond, and at times descended into little sheltered valleys close by the sea-side, with a smuggler's face scowling by us, and then had to ascend conical hills with a path winding up through a coppice to a barren top, like a monk's shaven crown, from one of which I pointed out to Coleridge's notice the bare masts of a vessel on the very edge of the horizon and within the red-orbed disk of the setting sun, like his own spectre-ship in the *Ancient Mariner.* At Linton the character of the sea-coast becomes more marked and rugged. There is a place called the *Valley of Rocks* (I suspect this was only the poetical name for it) bedded among precipices overhanging the sea, with rocky caverns beneath, into which the waves dash, and where the sea-gull for ever wheels its screaming flight. On the tops of these are huge stones thrown transverse, as if an earthquake had tossed them there, and behind these is a fretwork of perpendicular rocks, something like the *Giant's Causeway.* A thunder-storm came on while we were at the inn, and Coleridge was running out bareheaded to enjoy the commotion of the elements in the *Valley of Rocks,* but as if in spite, the clouds only muttered a few angry sounds, and let fall a few refreshing drops. Coleridge told me that he and Wordsworth were to have made this place the scene of a prose-tale, which was to have been in the manner of, but far superior to, the *Death of Abel,* but they had relinquished the design. In the morning of the second day, we breakfasted luxuriously in an old-fashioned parlour, on tea, toast, eggs, and honey, in the very sight of the bee-hives from which it had been taken, and a garden full of thyme and wild flowers that had produced it. On this occasion Coleridge spoke of Virgil's Georgics, but not well. I do not think he had much feeling for the classical or elegant. It was in this room that we found a little worn-out copy of the *Seasons;* lying in a window-seat, on which Coleridge exclaimed, " *That* is true fame!" He said Thomson was a great poet, rather than a good one; his style was as meretricious as his thoughts were natural. He spoke of Cowper as the best modern poet. He said the *Lyrical Ballads* were an experiment about to be tried by him and Wordsworth, to see how far the public taste would endure poetry written in a more natural and simple style than had hitherto been attempted ; . totally discarding the artifices of poetical diction, and making use only of such words as had probably been common in the most ordinary language since the days of Henry II. Some comparison was introduced between Shakespear and Milton. He said " he hardly knew which to prefer. Shakespear seemed to him a mere stripling in the art; he was as tall and as strong, with infinitely more activity than Milton, but he never appeared to have come to man's estate; or if he had, he would not have been a man, but a monster." He spoke with contempt of Gray, and with intolerance of Pope. He did not like the versification of the latter. He observed that " the ears of these couplet-writers might be charged with having short memories, that could not retain the harmony of whole passages." He thought little of Junius as a writer; he had a dislike of Dr. Johnson; and a much higher opinion of Burke as an orator and politician, than of Fox or Pitt. He however thought him very inferior in richness of style and imagery to some of our elder prose-writers, particularly Jeremy Taylor. He liked Richardson, but not Fielding; nor could I get him to enter into the merits of *Caleb Williams.** In short, he was profound and discriminating with

* He had no idea of pictures, of Claude or Raphael, and at this time I had as little as he. He sometimes gives a striking account at present of the Cartoons at Pisa, by Buffamalco and others; of one in particular, where Death is seen in the air brandishing his scythe, and the great and mighty of the earth

respect to those authors whom he liked, and where he gave his judgment fair play; capricious, perverse, and prejudiced in his antipathies and distastes. We loitered on the " ribbed sea-sands," in such talk as this, a whole morning, and I recollect met with a curious sea-weed, of which John Chester told us the country name! A fisherman gave Coleridge an account of a boy that had been drowned the day before, and that they had tried to save him at the risk of their own lives. He said " he did not know how it was that they ventured, but, Sir, we have a *nature* towards one another." This expression, Coleridge remarked to me, was a fine illustration of that theory of disinterestedness which I (in common with Butler) had adopted. I broached to him an argument of mine to prove that *likeness* was not mere association of ideas. I said that the mark in the sand put one in mind of a man's foot, not because it was part of a former impression of a man's foot (for it was quite new) but because it was like the shape of a man's foot. He assented to the justness of this distinction (which I have explained at length elsewhere, for the benefit of the curious) and John Chester listened; not from any interest in the subject, but because he was astonished that I should be able to suggest any thing to Coleridge that he did not already know. We returned on the third morning, and Coleridge remarked the silent cottage-smoke curling up the valleys where, a few evenings before, we had seen the lights gleaming through the dark.

In a day or two after we arrived at Stowey, we set out, I on my return home, and he for Germany. It was a Sunday morning, and he was to preach that day for Dr. Toulmin of Taunton. I asked him if he had prepared any thing for the

shudder at his approach, while the beggars and the wretched kneel to him as their deliverer. He would of course understand so broad and fine a moral as this at any time.

occasion? He said he had not even thought of the text, but should as soon as we parted. I did not go to hear him,—this was a fault,—but we met in the evening at Bridgewater. The next day we had a long day's walk to Bristol, and sat down, I recollect, by a well-side on the road, to cool ourselves and satisfy our thirst, when Coleridge repeated to me some descriptive lines from his tragedy of Remorse; which I must say became his mouth and that occasion better than they, some years after, did Mr. Elliston's and the Drury-lane boards,—

> " Oh memory! shield me from the world's poor strife,
> And give those scenes thine everlasting life."

I saw no more of him for a year or two, during which period he had been wandering in the Hartz Forest in Germany; and his return was cometary, meteorous, unlike his setting out. It was not till some time after that I knew his friends Lamb and Southey. The last always appears to me (as I first saw him) with a common-place book under his arm, and the first with a *bon-mot* in his mouth. It was at Godwin's that I met him with Holcroft and Coleridge, where they were disputing fiercely which was the best—*Man as he was, or man as he is to be.* " Give me," says Lamb, " man as he is *not* to be." This saying was the beginning of a friendship between us, which I believe still continues.— Enough of this for the present.

> " But there is matter for another rhyme,
> And I to this may add a second tale."

W. H.